WELCOME TO THE U.S.A.
SOUTH CAROLINA

Written by Ann Heinrichs   Illustrated by Matt Kania
Content Adviser: Tom Downey, PhD, Former Managing Editor
of the *South Carolina Encyclopedia*, Columbia, South Carolina

The Child's World

Published in the United States of America by The Child's World®
PO Box 326 • Chanhassen, MN 55317-0326
800-599-READ • www.childsworld.com

Photo Credits
Cover: Getty Images/Taxi/Colorstock; frontispiece: Susan Rosenthal/Corbis.

Interior: Catawba Cultural Preservation Project: 13; Corbis: 14 (Raymond Gehman), 18 (William A. Bake), 21 (Lee Snider/Photo Images), 26 (Bob Krist), 29 (Shepard Sherbell/Corbis Saba), 30 (James Marshall); Steve Franks/World Grits Festival: 33; David Muench/Corbis: 6, 22; South Carolina Department of Parks, Recreation, and Tourism: 9, 10, 17, 25; Town of Salley: 34.

Acknowledgments
The Child's World®: Mary Berendes, Publishing Director

Editorial Directions, Inc.: Editorial Directions, Inc.: E. Russell Primm, Editorial Director; Katie Marsico, Associate Editor; Judith Shiffer, Assistant Editor; Matt Messbarger, Editorial Assistant; Susan Hindman, Copy Editor; Melissa McDaniel, Proofreader; Kevin Cunningham, Peter Garnham, Matt Messbarger, Olivia Nellums, Chris Simms, Molly Symmonds, Katherine Trickle, Carl Stephen Wender, Fact Checkers; Tim Griffin/IndexServ, Indexer; Cian Loughlin O'Day, Photo Researcher and Editor

The Design Lab: Kathleen Petelinsek, Design; Julia Goozen, Art Production

Library of Congress Cataloging-in-Publication Data
Heinrichs, Ann.
  South Carolina / by Ann Heinrichs ; cartography and illustrations by Matt Kania.
    p. cm. — (Welcome to the U.S.A.)
  Includes index.
  ISBN 1-59296-482-6 (library bound : alk. paper)
  1. South Carolina—Juvenile literature. I. Kania, Matt, ill. II. Title.
  F269.3.H45 2006
  975.7—dc22   2005010502

About the Author
Ann Heinrichs

Ann Heinrichs is the author of more than 100 books for children and young adults. She has also enjoyed successful careers as a children's book editor and an advertising copywriter. Ann grew up in Fort Smith, Arkansas, and lives in Chicago, Illinois.

About the Map Illustrator
Matt Kania

Matt Kania loves maps and, as a kid, dreamed of making them. In school he studied geography and cartography, and today he makes maps for a living. Matt's favorite thing about drawing maps is learning about the places they represent. Many of the maps he has created can be found in books, magazines, videos, Web sites, and public places.

On the cover: **The Isle of Palms is a great place to enjoy the beach.**
On page one: **Many different plants and animals call The Audubon Swamp Garden at Magnolia Plantation home.**

OUR SOUTH CAROLINA TRIP

South Carolina's Nickname:
The Palmetto State

4

Ready to explore the Palmetto State? Then hop aboard. We're heading for South Carolina! Just follow that loopy dotted line. Or else skip around. Either way, you're in for a great adventure.

You'll meet tree frogs, sea turtles, and otters. You'll see sand dunes and waterfalls. You'll learn about battles that shaped the nation. You'll eat chitlins and grits. And you'll visit two very different factories. One makes cars. The other is a goat farm!

Are you curious? Then buckle up and hang on tight. We're off!

WELCOME
TO SOUTH
CAROLINA

NORTH CAROLINA

Chesnee

Sumter National Forest

Greenville

85

Rock Hill

77

McBee

26

Sumter National Forest

Sumter National Forest

Greenwood

Columbia

SOUTH CAROLINA

95

Myrtle Beach

20

Salley

Georgetown

GEORGIA

Savannah River

Saint George

Charleston

As you travel through South Carolina, watch for all the interesting facts along the way.

Beaufort

ATLANTIC OCEAN

What's that thundering sound? It's Whitewater Falls! It's the highest waterfall in the eastern United States.

Looking for a good spot to canoe? Check out the Chattooga River!

Sumter National Forest in the Blue Ridge Region

Paddle your canoe down the Chattooga River. It twists and turns through the forest. Or take a hiking trail. You'll pass beautiful waterfalls.

You're enjoying Sumter National Forest. The forest is in three different parts in South Carolina's northwest corner. The Blue Ridge Mountains run through this area. The hilly Piedmont Region slopes down from there. South Carolina's hilly regions are called the upcountry.

The lowcountry is the state's largest region. It's a wide coastal plain. Southeastern South Carolina faces the Atlantic Ocean. Many areas near the coast are **swamps.**

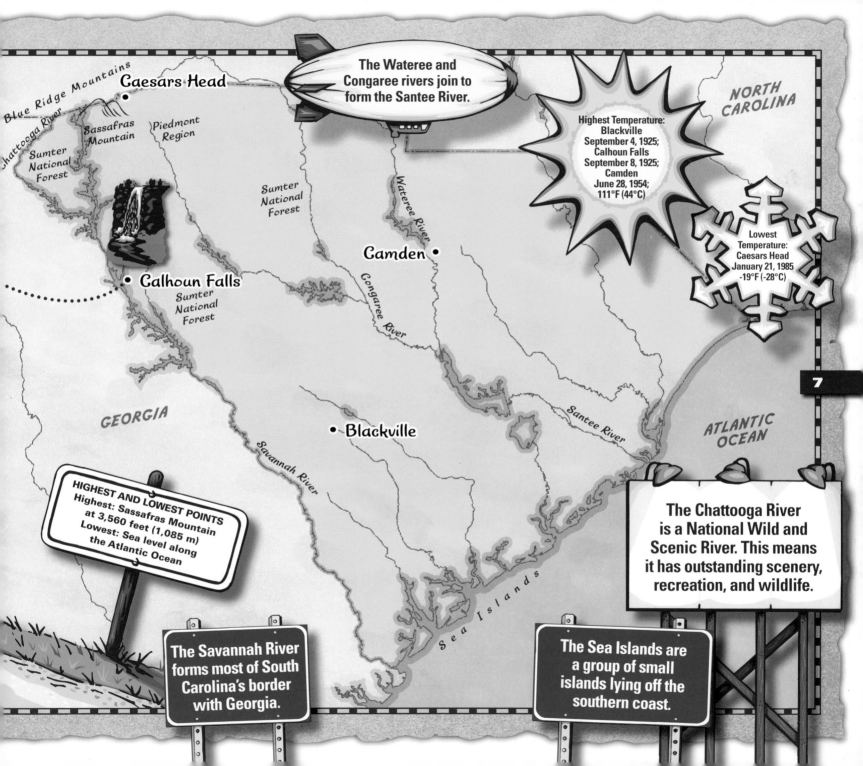

Blue Ridge Mountains

Chattooga River

Caesars Head

Sassafras Mountain

Piedmont Region

Sumter National Forest

The Wateree and Congaree rivers join to form the Santee River.

NORTH CAROLINA

Highest Temperature: Blackville September 4, 1925; Calhoun Falls September 8, 1925; Camden June 28, 1954; 111°F (44°C)

Sumter National Forest

Wateree River

Camden

Lowest Temperature: Caesars Head January 21, 1985 -19°F (-28°C)

Calhoun Falls

Sumter National Forest

Congaree River

GEORGIA

Santee River

ATLANTIC OCEAN

Blackville

Savannah River

HIGHEST AND LOWEST POINTS
Highest: Sassafras Mountain at 3,560 feet (1,085 m)
Lowest: Sea level along the Atlantic Ocean

The Chattooga River is a National Wild and Scenic River. This means it has outstanding scenery, recreation, and wildlife.

Sea Islands

The Savannah River forms most of South Carolina's border with Georgia.

The Sea Islands are a group of small islands lying off the southern coast.

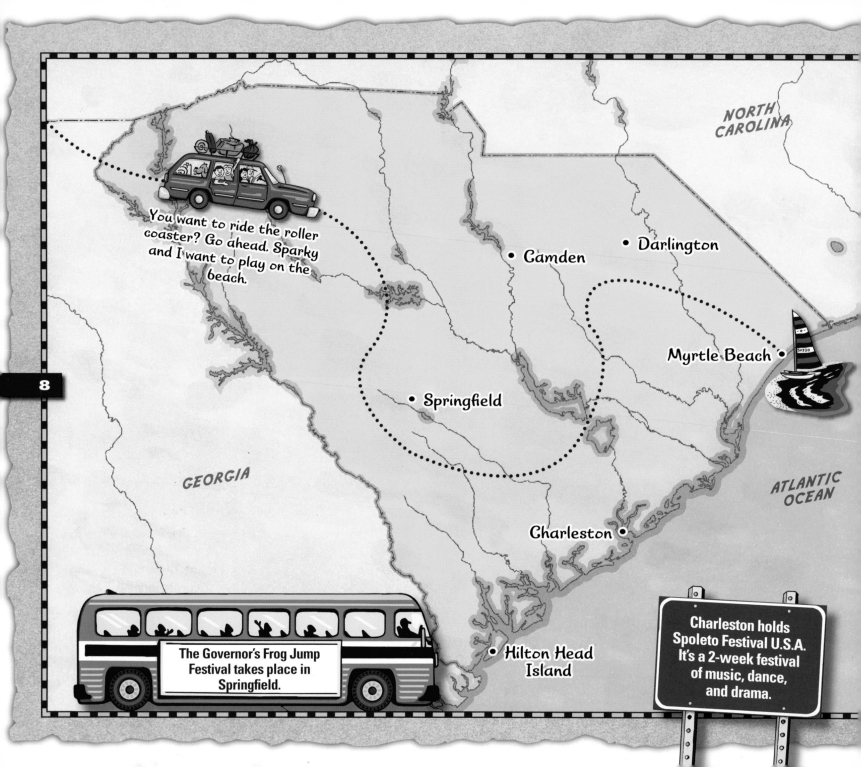

You want to ride the roller coaster? Go ahead. Sparky and I want to play on the beach.

• Camden

• Darlington

Myrtle Beach •

• Springfield

GEORGIA

ATLANTIC OCEAN

NORTH CAROLINA

Charleston •

• Hilton Head Island

The Governor's Frog Jump Festival takes place in Springfield.

Charleston holds Spoleto Festival U.S.A. It's a 2-week festival of music, dance, and drama.

Fun at Myrtle Beach

Admire the sand dunes. Gather some seashells. Catch a fish. Or maybe you like noisy fun. Then hop on a ride at the amusement park. You can do it all at Myrtle Beach!

Many popular beaches line South Carolina's coast. Myrtle Beach is on the northeast coast. Hilton Head Island is a favorite spot, too. It's just off the southeast coast.

South Carolina's also a great place for racing. Camden holds the Carolina Cup horse race. Darlington is known for its car races. And there are sailboat races off the coast.

Make a splash at South Carolina's famous beaches!

Myrtle Beach holds the Sun Fun Festival in June. It features beach games, an air show, and other fun events.

Forests cover more than half of South Carolina.

Yikes! Alligators are right at home in coastal South Carolina.

Carolina Sandhills National Wildlife Refuge is one of the best places to bird-watch in the whole state!

Carolina Sandhills National Wildlife Refuge near McBee

You'll love exploring Carolina Sandhills National Wildlife Refuge. There's so much going on!

Do you hear a chirping sound? It's a little green tree frog. You may see fox squirrels on the ground. People sometimes mistake them for foxes!

Do you hear a slapping sound? It's a beaver. Beavers slap their wide tails on the water. It's a warning sound for other beavers. You may see river otters in the water. They swim on their backs. Their webbed feet help them swim. Alligators live in the coastal swamps. Dolphins, sharks, and whales swim offshore. Sea turtles come ashore to build nests.

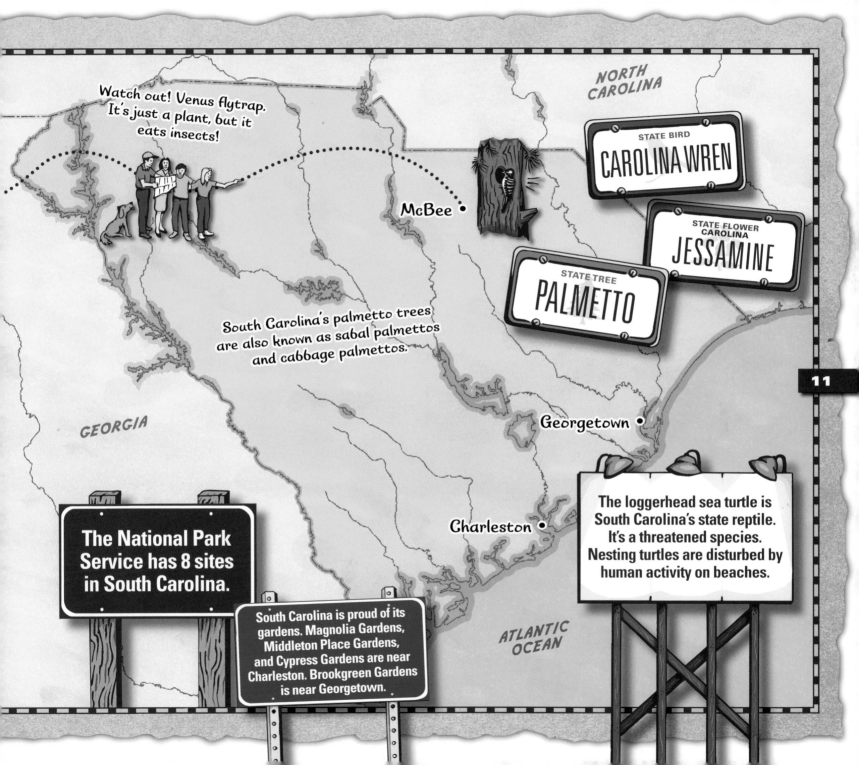

Watch out! Venus flytrap. It's just a plant, but it eats insects!

NORTH CAROLINA

McBee

South Carolina's palmetto trees are also known as sabal palmettos and cabbage palmettos.

GEORGIA

STATE BIRD
CAROLINA WREN

STATE FLOWER
CAROLINA
JESSAMINE

STATE TREE
PALMETTO

Georgetown

Charleston

ATLANTIC OCEAN

The National Park Service has 8 sites in South Carolina.

South Carolina is proud of its gardens. Magnolia Gardens, Middleton Place Gardens, and Cypress Gardens are near Charleston. Brookgreen Gardens is near Georgetown.

The loggerhead sea turtle is South Carolina's state reptile. It's a threatened species. Nesting turtles are disturbed by human activity on beaches.

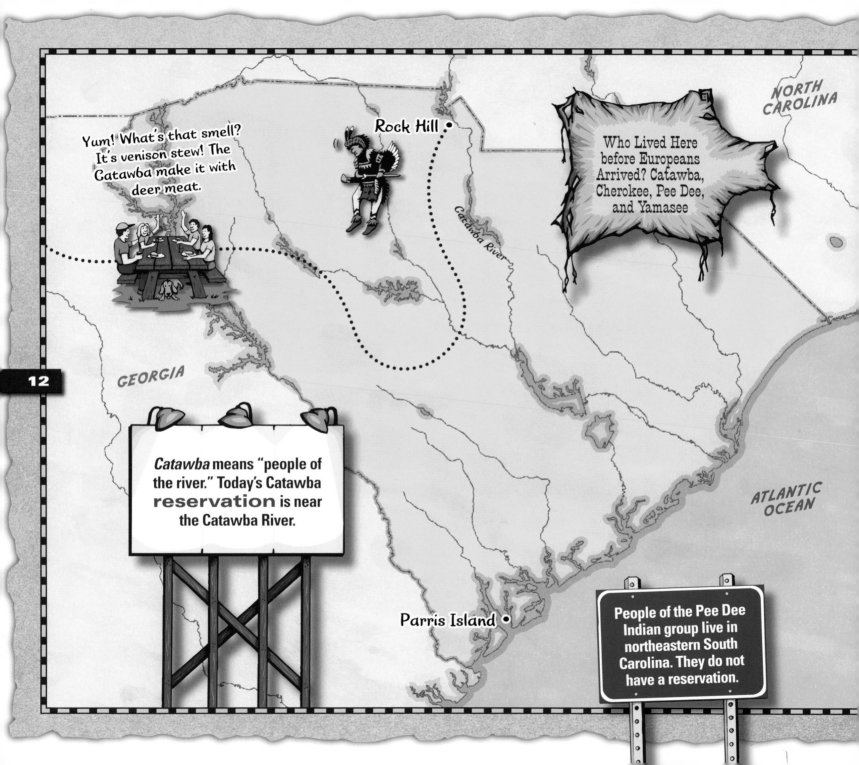

The Day of the Catawba at Rock Hill

The dancers all wear traditional dress. Feathers and fringe swirl with each movement. These Native American performers are Catawba people. They're celebrating *Yap Ye Iswa*. That means "Day of the Catawba."

Thousands of Indians once lived in South Carolina. The Catawba knew which plants to use as medicine. They passed on their history through storytelling.

Spanish explorers arrived in the 1500s. Spaniards tried to establish a **colony** in 1526. They left after a few months, though. French **colonists** came in 1562. They soon left, too. Spaniards returned in 1566. They established Santa Elena on Parris Island.

Yap Ye Iswa is a celebration of Catawba culture.

What were ships like in the 1600s? Visit Charles Towne Landing and find out!

Charles Towne was named after King Charles II of England.

Charles Towne Landing

Climb aboard the *Adventure*. It's built just like the colonists' trading ships. Then stroll through the village. It's just like a colonial town in the 1600s.

You're exploring Charles Towne Landing. English colonists settled here in 1670. In 1680, they moved to Oyster Point. This became Charleston, South Carolina's first permanent town.

South Carolina's early settlers lived near the coast. Many of them grew rice. They sent their products out on ships. Charleston grew to be a busy port city.

A group of English noblemen set up the Carolina Colony. The colony split in 1729. It became North Carolina and South Carolina.

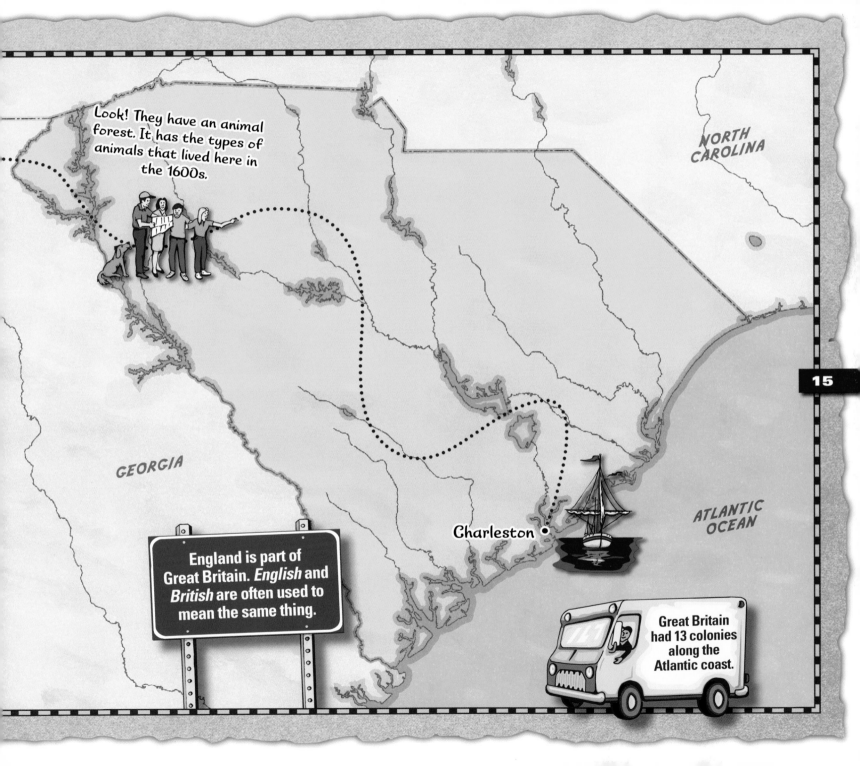

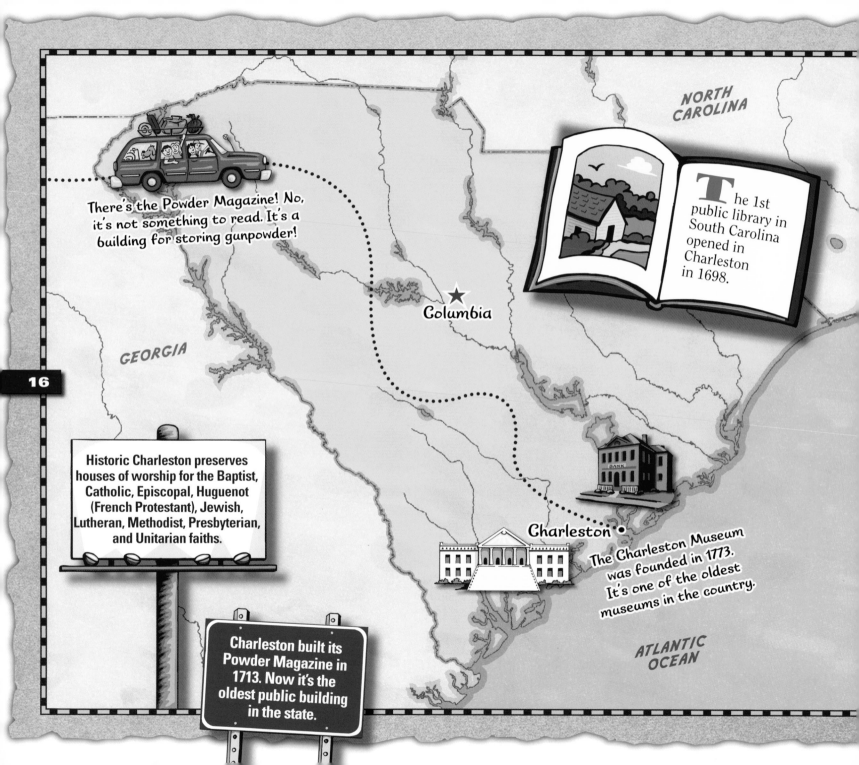

NORTH CAROLINA

There's the Powder Magazine! No, it's not something to read. It's a building for storing gunpowder!

The 1st public library in South Carolina opened in Charleston in 1698.

GEORGIA

Columbia

Historic Charleston preserves houses of worship for the Baptist, Catholic, Episcopal, Huguenot (French Protestant), Jewish, Lutheran, Methodist, Presbyterian, and Unitarian faiths.

Charleston

The Charleston Museum was founded in 1773. It's one of the oldest museums in the country.

Charleston built its Powder Magazine in 1713. Now it's the oldest public building in the state.

ATLANTIC OCEAN

Historic Charleston

Would you like to step back 300 years? That's easy. Just visit Charleston's historic district. It preserves many buildings from Charleston's early days.

Charleston was a wealthy city in the 1700s. Ships sailed in and out of its port. The Exchange Building still stands today. Merchants handled their shipping business there.

Some ships brought in people from Africa. They were sold in the marketplace as slaves. You can still see the Old Slave Mart. Another historic building is Market Hall. People sold fresh vegetables and meat there.

How did people get around before cars? Take a carriage ride through historic Charleston.

Charleston was South Carolina's capital until 1790. Then Columbia became the capital.

Travel back in time! This monument recalls the Battle of Cowpens.

South Carolina was the 8th state to enter the Union. It joined on May 23, 1788.

Cowpens National Battlefield near Chesnee

In time, the colonists wanted their freedom. They fought Great Britain in the Revolutionary War (1775–1783).

Colonial troops won some big victories in South Carolina. One victory was at the Battle of Cowpens. You can visit the battlefield today. Exhibits at the visitors' center explain what happened.

Special events take place on the battle's anniversary. People dress like Revolutionary War soldiers. They show how the colonists fired their guns.

The war was hard, but the colonists were tough. They won! The colonies became the United States of America.

Blacksburg

Chesnee

How did Cowpens get its name? Early Carolina farmers allowed cattle and other animals to roam free. In fall, local herders used to round the animals up into structures called cow pens.

The Battle of Cowpens took place on January 17, 1781. The battle site is now a national battlefield.

GEORGIA

British forces captured Charleston in 1780. They left in 1782.

The Battle of Kings Mountain took place near Blacksburg in 1780. The colonists won an important victory there.

Charleston

Sullivan's Island

ATLANTIC OCEAN

Fort Moultrie was originally built of palmetto logs. A palmetto tree is on the state flag. It honors the colonists' successful defense of the fort.

Fort Moultrie is on Sullivan's Island. The colonists defended this fort against British warships in 1776.

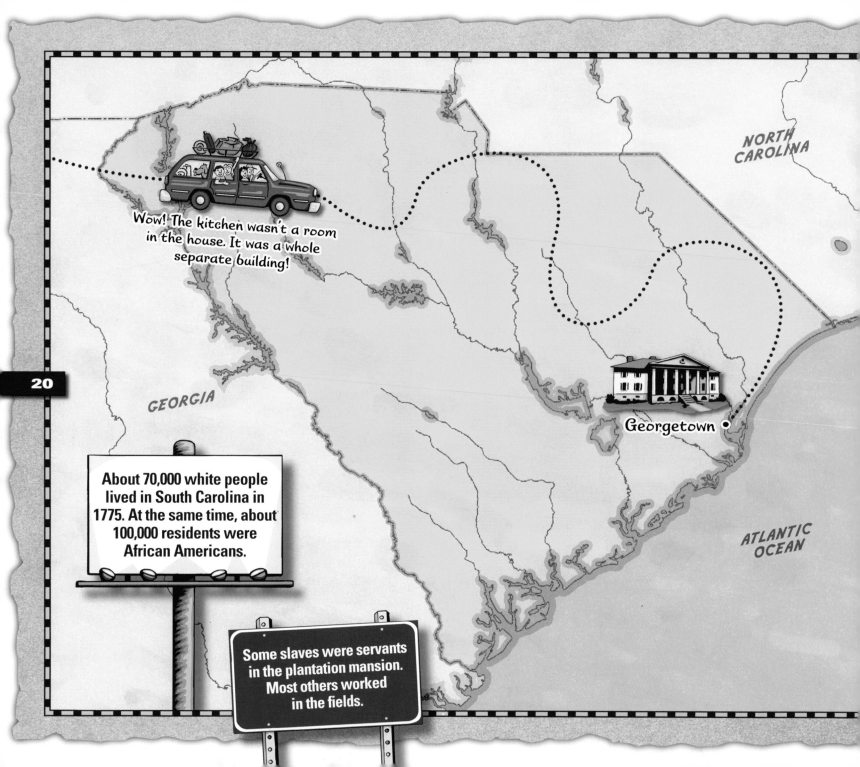

Wow! The kitchen wasn't a room in the house. It was a whole separate building!

NORTH CAROLINA

GEORGIA

Georgetown

About 70,000 white people lived in South Carolina in 1775. At the same time, about 100,000 residents were African Americans.

ATLANTIC OCEAN

Some slaves were servants in the plantation mansion. Most others worked in the fields.

Hampton Plantation near Georgetown

Wander through the elegant **mansion.** Stroll through the fields. Things are quiet at Hampton **Plantation** now. But it was once bustling with activity.

Hampton Plantation grew rice. That was South Carolina's leading crop in the 1700s. Coastal farmers still raised rice into the 1800s. By the mid-1800s, cotton was the major crop. African American slaves worked on the plantations.

Northern and Southern states argued about slavery. Most Southerners were in favor of slavery. But many Northerners were against it. This conflict would grow into a war.

How did South Carolinans live in the 1700s? Tour Hampton Plantation and find out!

Hampton Plantation began operating in about 1750.

Fort Sumter in Charleston Harbor

Cannons still stand around Fort Sumter. You reach this island fort by boat.

Slavery was a growing issue among the states. Finally, South Carolina pulled away from the Union. Other Southern states followed. They formed the Confederate States of America.

U.S. troops occupied Fort Sumter. On April 12, 1861, Confederates fired on the fort. Union troops were forced to surrender. That began the Civil War (1861–1865).

Union general William Sherman marched through South Carolina. His soldiers burned Columbia and many plantations. In the end, the Union won the war.

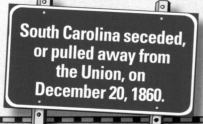

Boom! Check out this cannon at Fort Sumter!

South Carolina seceded, or pulled away from the Union, on December 20, 1860.

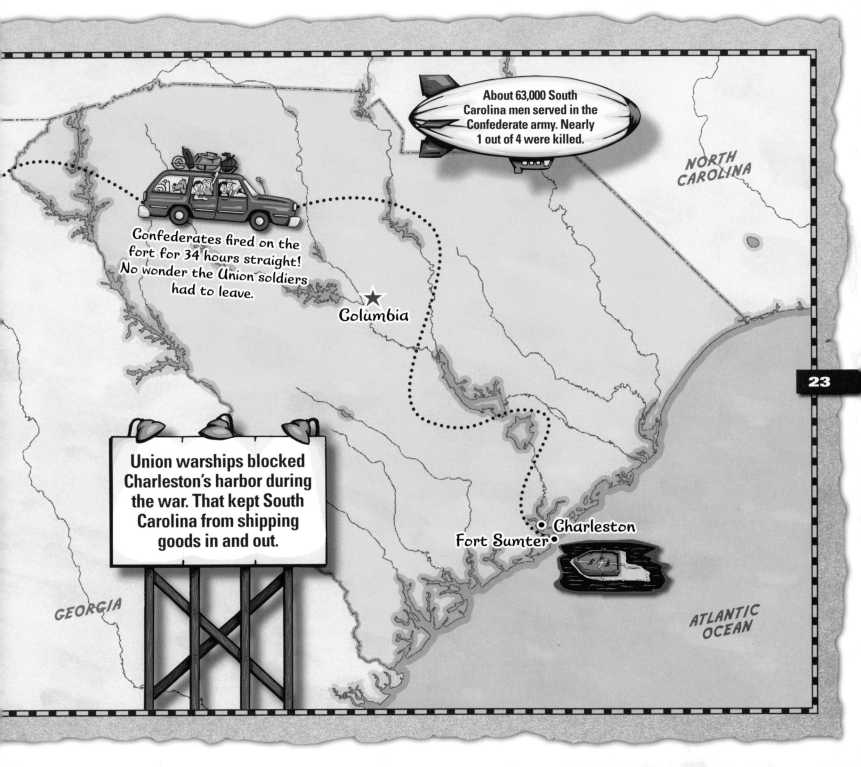

About 63,000 South Carolina men served in the Confederate army. Nearly 1 out of 4 were killed.

Confederates fired on the fort for 34 hours straight! No wonder the Union soldiers had to leave.

Union warships blocked Charleston's harbor during the war. That kept South Carolina from shipping goods in and out.

NORTH CAROLINA

Columbia

Fort Sumter • Charleston

GEORGIA

ATLANTIC OCEAN

Look at all those stars! The capitol really took a beating!

The South Carolina State Museum is in Columbia. It has exhibits on art, history, science, and technology.

NORTH CAROLINA

GEORGIA

Columbia

ATLANTIC OCEAN

Strom Thurmond (1902–2003) was a U.S. senator from South Carolina (1955–2003). He retired as the oldest member of Congress. He also served longer in the Senate than anyone else.

Welcome to Columbia, the capital of South Carolina!

South Carolina has 2 state mottoes. One is *Amimis Opibusque Parati.* This is Latin for "Prepared in Mind and Resources." The second is *Dum Spiro Spero.* This is Latin for "While I Breathe, I Hope."

The State Capitol in Columbia

Stroll around the outside of the capitol. Keep your eyes on the wall. Here and there, you'll see metal stars. They're a reminder of Civil War days. In 1865, Union soldiers fired cannons on the capitol. The stars mark the spots where cannonballs struck.

Inside the capitol are state government offices. South Carolina's government is divided into three branches. One branch makes the state's laws. Another branch carries out those laws. It's headed by the governor. The third branch is made up of judges. They decide whether someone has broken the law.

South Carolina lawmakers are hard at work inside the capitol.

Woodrow Wilson was the 28th president (1913–1921). He lived in Columbia for 4 years as a teenager. You can visit his boyhood home there.

Beaufort's Gullah Festival

Catch the beat! Drummers perform at the Gullah Festival.

Shouts and drumbeats fill the air. Dancers in colorful African costumes whirl and sway. You're watching the Gullah Festival!

This festival celebrates the **culture** of the Gullah people. They live on South Carolina's Sea Islands. The Gullah are descended from West African slaves. They keep much of their culture alive. That includes their language, storytelling, music, and dances.

Ancestors of the Gullah people came from many West African countries, including Senegal and Sierra Leone.

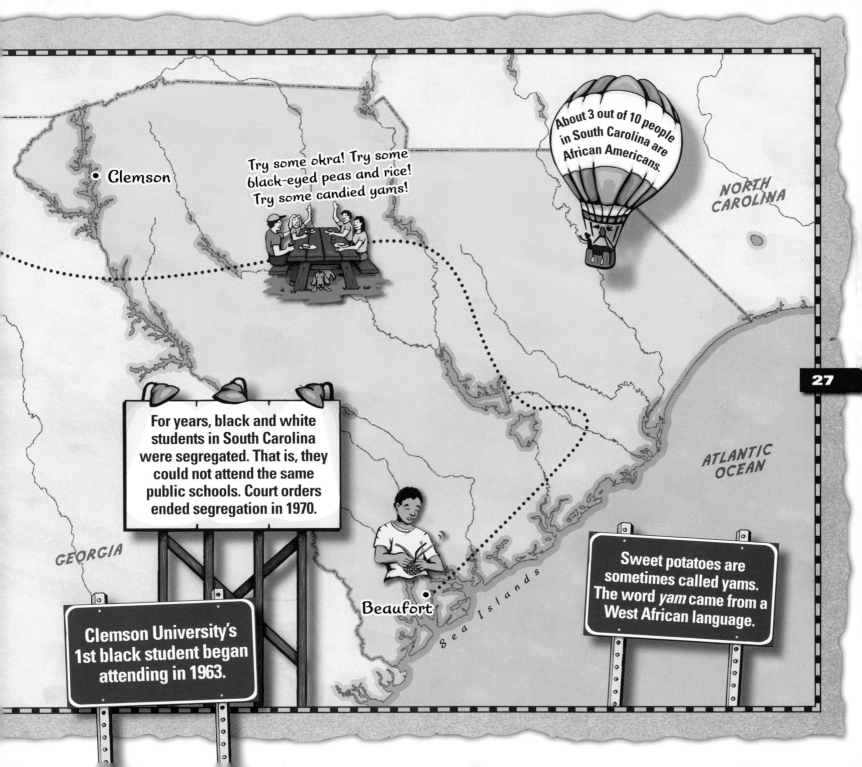

Try some okra! Try some black-eyed peas and rice! Try some candied yams!

About 3 out of 10 people in South Carolina are African Americans.

For years, black and white students in South Carolina were segregated. That is, they could not attend the same public schools. Court orders ended segregation in 1970.

Clemson University's 1st black student began attending in 1963.

Sweet potatoes are sometimes called yams. The word *yam* came from a West African language.

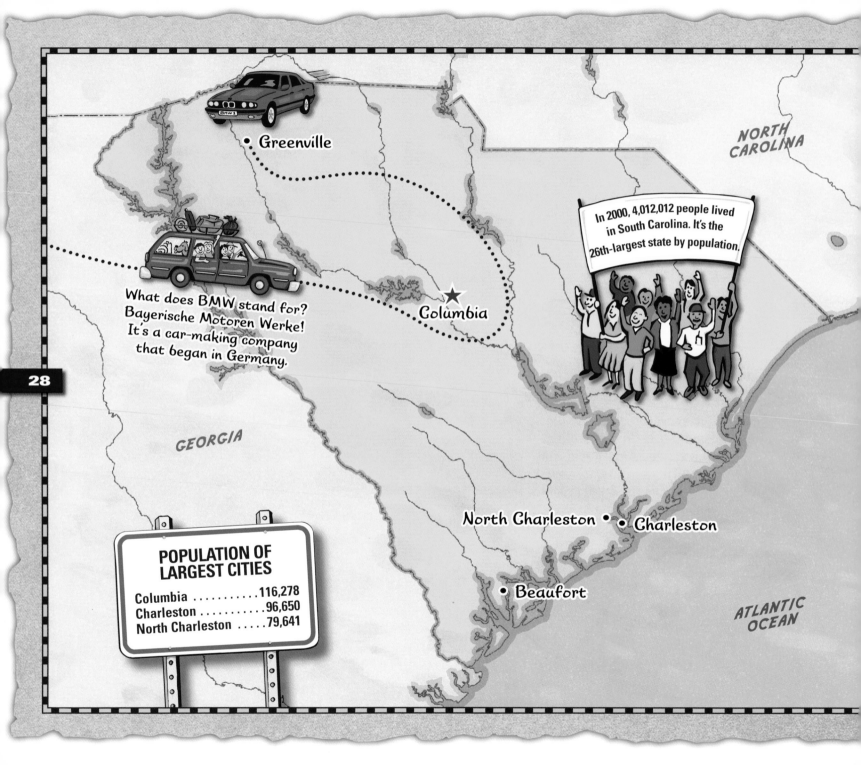

Greenville

What does BMW stand for?
Bayerische Motoren Werke!
It's a car-making company
that began in Germany.

In 2000, 4,012,012 people lived
in South Carolina. It's the
26th-largest state by population.

NORTH
CAROLINA

Columbia

GEORGIA

North Charleston • • Charleston

• Beaufort

ATLANTIC
OCEAN

**POPULATION OF
LARGEST CITIES**

Columbia 116,278
Charleston 96,650
North Charleston 79,641

Touring the BMW Factory near Greenville

The BMW company began in 1916 in Munich, Germany.

Some workers are **welding** metals. They wear masks to protect their faces. Others work at long lines of machinery. Finally, out come the finished products. Shiny new cars!

You're touring the BMW car plant. It's one of the state's many busy factories.

Manufacturing grew after the Civil War. Many textile mills opened in the late 1800s. They turned raw cotton into cloth.

More new factories sprang up. By the mid-1950s, the state had changed. More people worked in factories than on farms!

Do you want to own a BMW someday? Stop by the BMW plant in Greenville!

Need a bar of soap? Look no farther than the goats of Emerald Farm!

In 1910, South Carolina had 167 textile mills. About 50,000 people worked in the mills. They made cotton cloth.

Emerald Farm in Greenwood

Looking for a really unusual factory tour? This one is on a goat farm!

Emerald Farm raises goats. The farm has a soap factory. It makes soap out of goat's milk! You're welcome to visit the farm. You can pet the goats. Then watch how the soap is made.

South Carolina factories make much more than soap. The leading factory goods are chemicals. They include plastics and medicines. Textiles, or cloth, are important, too. Some factories make cotton, silk, or wool cloth. Others make polyester, rayon, or nylon. Paper and machines are some other factory goods.

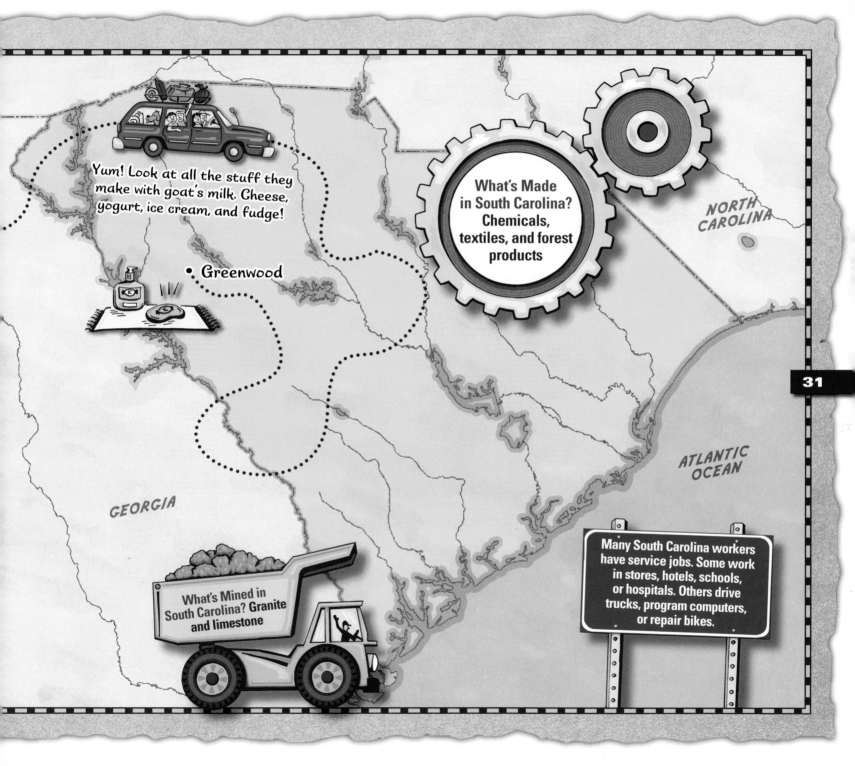

Yum! Look at all the stuff they make with goat's milk. Cheese, yogurt, ice cream, and fudge!

• Greenwood

What's Made in South Carolina? Chemicals, textiles, and forest products

NORTH CAROLINA

GEORGIA

ATLANTIC OCEAN

What's Mined in South Carolina? Granite and limestone

Many South Carolina workers have service jobs. Some work in stores, hotels, schools, or hospitals. Others drive trucks, program computers, or repair bikes.

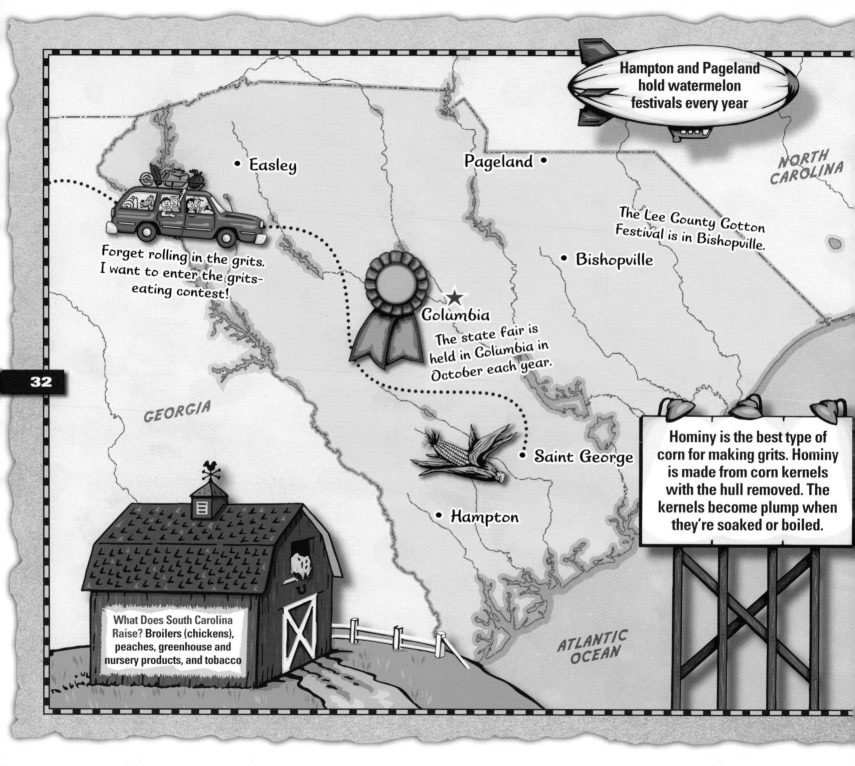

Hampton and Pageland hold watermelon festivals every year

• Easley

Pageland •

NORTH CAROLINA

The Lee County Cotton Festival is in Bishopville.

• Bishopville

Forget rolling in the grits. I want to enter the grits-eating contest!

★ Columbia

The state fair is held in Columbia in October each year.

GEORGIA

Hominy is the best type of corn for making grits. Hominy is made from corn kernels with the hull removed. The kernels become plump when they're soaked or boiled.

• Saint George

• Hampton

What Does South Carolina Raise? Broilers (chickens), peaches, greenhouse and nursery products, and tobacco

ATLANTIC OCEAN

The World Grits Festival in Saint George

First you get weighed. Then you plunge into a pool of grits. That's a mush of ground-up corn kernels. You **wallow** around for ten seconds. Then you get weighed again. You're hoping lots of grits stuck to you. Whoever gains the most weight is the winner!

You're in the Rolling in the Grits Contest. It's a fun event at the World Grits Festival!

South Carolina has plenty of grits to eat. Corn is a big crop in the state. Tobacco is the top crop, though. Shrubs and flowers are important crops, too. Chickens bring in even more income than crops. Farmers also raise turkeys, cattle, and hogs.

Talk about playing with your food! Be sure to enter the Rolling in the Grits Contest!

Golden Creek Mill in Easley is a restored 1825 mill with a waterwheel. It grinds cornmeal, grits, and flour.

KiDS NEED a **STABLE** BackGr

It's parade time! People of all ages take part in the Chitlin Strut parade.

Salley's Chitlin Strut

Put on your hog hat. You'll fit right in at the Chitlin Strut parade!

The Chitlin Strut is a big food festival. It takes place in the tiny town of Salley. Thousands of people show up every year. But what are chitlins?

Chitlins are a **traditional** Southern food. The word *chitlins* is short for chitterlings. They're hog intestines, boiled and deep-fried—yum!

South Carolina has lots of food festivals. Beaufort is known for its shrimp festival. Mount Pleasant holds a seafood festival every year. It also hosts the Lowcountry Oyster Festival. It's called the world's largest oyster roast!

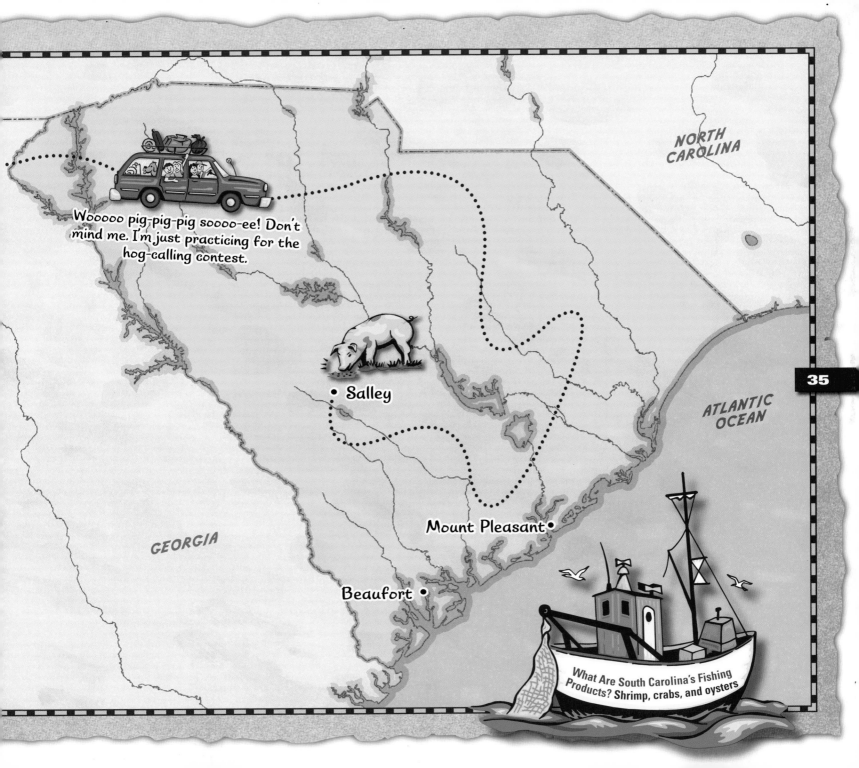

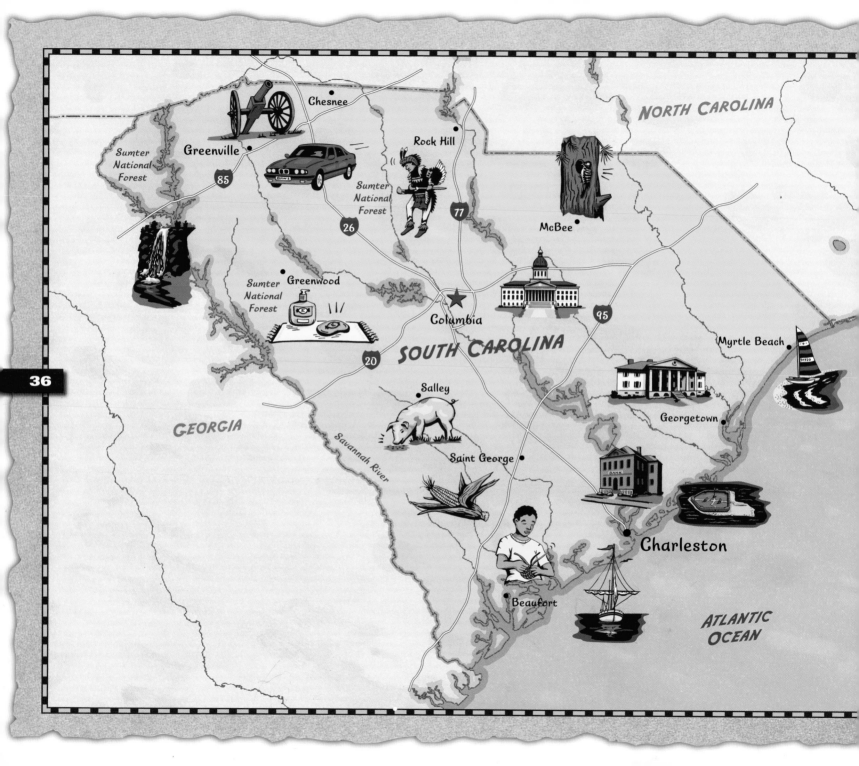

NORTH CAROLINA

Sumter National Forest

Chesnee

Greenville

Rock Hill

McBee

85

26

77

Sumter National Forest

Greenwood

Sumter National Forest

Columbia

SOUTH CAROLINA

95

Myrtle Beach

20

Salley

GEORGIA

Savannah River

Saint George

Georgetown

Charleston

Beaufort

ATLANTIC OCEAN

OUR TRIP

We visited many amazing places on our trip! We also met a lot of interesting people along the way. Look at the map on the left. Use your finger to trace all the places we have been.

What forms most of South Carolina's border with Georgia? See page 7 for the answer.

Where is the Sun Fun Festival held? Page 9 has the answer.

What does the word *Catawba* mean? See page 12 for the answer.

Who was Charles Towne named after? Look on page 14 for the answer.

What is South Carolina's oldest public building? Page 16 has the answer.

What year did Columbia become South Carolina's capital? Turn to page 17 for the answer.

What U.S. senator served the longest? Look on page 24 to find out!

What is the best type of corn for making grits? Turn to page 32 for the answer.

That was a great trip! We have traveled all over South Carolina!

There are a few places that we didn't have time for, though. Next time, we plan to visit Ripley's Aquarium in Myrtle Beach. Visitors can see 10-foot (3-m) sharks and other amazing sea life. Scientists even conduct hourly dives and marine education classes!

More Places to Visit in South Carolina

WORDS TO KNOW

colonists (KOL-uh-nists) people who settle a new land for their home country

colony (KOL-uh-nee) a land with ties to a mother country

culture (KUHL-chur) a group of people's customs and ways of life

mansion (MAN-shuhn) a large, elegant house

plantation (plan-TAY-shuhn) a large farm that raises mainly 1 crop

reservation (rez-ur-VAY-shuhn) land set aside for a special use, such as for Native Americans

swamps (SWAHMPS) wetlands

traditional (truh-DISH-uhn-ul) following long-held customs

wallow (WOL-oh) to roll around in something such as mud

welding (WELD-ing) joining metal parts by applying intense heat

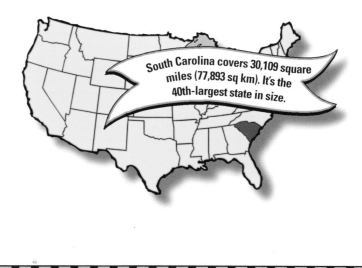

South Carolina covers 30,109 square miles (77,893 sq km). It's the 40th-largest state in size.

STATE SYMBOLS

State animal: White-tailed deer

State beverage: Milk

State bird: Carolina wren

State botanical garden: Botanical Garden at Clemson University

State dance: Shag

State dog: Boykin spaniel

State fish: Striped bass

State flower: Carolina jessamine

State fruit: Peach

State gemstone: Amethyst

State insect: Carolina mantid (praying mantis)

State reptile: Loggerhead sea turtle

State shell: Lettered olive

State stone: Blue granite

State tree: Palmetto

State wild game bird: Wild turkey

State flag

State seal

STATE SONG

"Carolina"

Words by Henry Timrod, music by Anne Curtis Burgess

Call on thy children of the hill,
Wake swamp and river, coast and rill,
Rouse all thy strength and all thy skill,
Carolina! Carolina!

Hold up the glories of thy dead;
Say how thy elder children bled,
And point to Eutaw's battle-bed,
Carolina! Carolina!

Thy skirts indeed the foe may part,
Thy robe be pierced with sword and dart,
They shall not touch thy noble heart,
Carolina! Carolina!

Throw thy bold banner to the breeze!
Front with thy ranks the threatening seas
Like thine own proud armorial trees,
Carolina! Carolina!

Girt with such wills to do and bear,
Assured in right, and mailed in prayer,
Thou wilt not bow thee to despair,
Carolina! Carolina!

FAMOUS PEOPLE

Anderson, Bill (1937–), country singer

Baldwin, James Mark (1861–1934), psychologist

Baruch, Bernard (1870–1965), businessman and statesman

Bethune, Mary McLeod (1875–1955), educator

Brown, James (1933–), singer

Byars, Betsy (1928–), children's author

Calhoun, John C. (1782–1850), statesman

Frazier, Joe (1944–), boxer

Gibson, Althea (1927–2003), tennis player

Gillespie, John Birks "Dizzy" (1917–1993), jazz musician

Heyward, DuBose (1885–1940), poet, author, playwright

Hunter-Gault, Charlayne (1942–), journalist

Jackson, Andrew (1767–1845), 7th U.S. president

Jackson, Jesse (1941–), civil rights leader

Jackson, "Shoeless" Joe (1888–1951), baseball player

Kitt, Eartha (1927–), singer, actor

McNair, Ronald (1950–1986), astronaut

Thurmond, Strom (1902–2003), senator

Townes, Charles H. (1915–), physicist

White, Vanna (1957–), TV performer

TO FIND OUT MORE

At the Library
Blashfield, Jean. *The South Carolina Colony.* Chanhassen, Minn.: The Child's World, 2004.

Burke, Rick. *Andrew Jackson.* Chicago: Heinemann Library, 2003.

Crane, Carol, and Mary Whyte (illustrator). *P Is for Palmetto: A South Carolina Alphabet.* Chelsea, Mich.: Sleeping Bear Press, 2002.

Jones, Amy Robin. *Mary McLeod Bethune.* Chanhassen, Minn.: The Child's World, 2001.

On the Web
Visit our home page for lots of links about South Carolina: *http://www.childsworld.com/links*

Note to Parents, Teachers, and Librarians: We routinely verify our Web links to make sure they are safe, active sites—so encourage your readers to check them out!

Places to Visit or Contact
South Carolina Department of Parks, Recreation, and Tourism
1205 Pendleton Street, Room 505
Columbia, SC 29201
803/734-1700
For more information about traveling in South Carolina

The South Carolina Historical Society
The Fireproof Building
100 Meeting Street
Charleston, SC 29401
843/723-3225
For more information about the history of South Carolina

INDEX

Bye, Palmetto State.
We had a great time.
We'll come back soon!